AQUARIUM

BY K.C. KELLEY

AMICUS READERS ● AMICUS INK

amicus
readers

Amicus Readers and Amicus Ink are imprints of Amicus
P.O. Box 1329, Mankato, MN 56002
www.amicuspublishing.us

Library of Congress Cataloging-in-Publication Data

Names: Kelley, K. C., author.
Title: Aquarium / by K.C. Kelley.
Description: Mankato, MN : Amicus, [2018] | Series: Field trips, let's go!
Identifiers: LCCN 2017022577 (print) | LCCN 2017034679 (ebook) | ISBN
  9781681513386 (pdf) | ISBN 9781681513027 (library binding : alk. paper) |
  ISBN 9781681522586 (pbk. : alk. paper)
Subjects: LCSH: Aquariums--Juvenile literature. | Aquarium fishes--Juvenile
  literature.
Classification: LCC SF457.25 (ebook) | LCC SF457.25 .K45 2018 (print) | DDC
  639.34--dc23
LC record available at https://lccn.loc.gov/2017022577

Editor: Sara Frederick
Designer: Patty Kelley
Photo Researcher/Producer: Shoreline Publishing Group LLC

Photo Credits:
Cover: Brad Calkins/Dreamstime.com
Adobe Stock: Pavel Losevsky 3, Olesia Bilkei 6; Alamy Stock: Image Source Sales 9; Dreamstime.com: Feverpitched 5, Paulus Rusyanto 10, Ian Mcdonald 13, Bexcellent 16T, Argus12 16B, Wrangel 16R. Shutterstock: Paolo OK 15.

Printed in China.

HC 10 9 8 7 6 5 4 3 2 1
PB 10 9 8 7 6 5 4 3 2 1

Let's go to the aquarium!
Fish live there.

The fish live in big tanks. The tanks are full of water. Tina spots a shark.

Fish come in all sizes. Andy loves the bright colors.

Sea animals can
be many shapes.
Donna finds
a seashell.

Other sea
animals live here.

Sara sees a penguin.

Penguins breathe air.

They are great

swimmers.

Workers feed
the fish.
That looks like fun!
Kendra waves
to the diver.

What a great day at the aquarium! What was your favorite animal?

THINGS TO SEE AT AN AQUARIUM

manta ray

crab

octopus